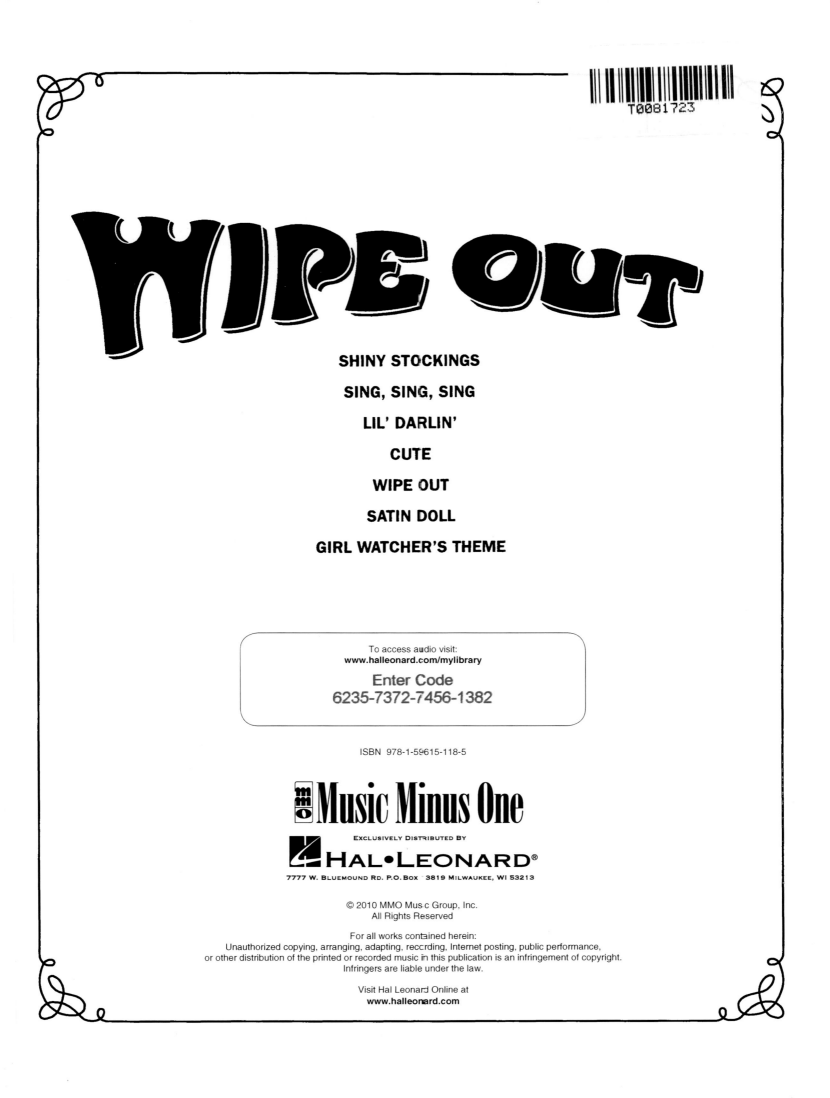

WIPE OUT

SHINY STOCKINGS

SING, SING, SING

LIL' DARLIN'

CUTE

WIPE OUT

SATIN DOLL

GIRL WATCHER'S THEME

To access audio visit:
www.halleonard.com/mylibrary

Enter Code
6235-7372-7456-1382

ISBN 978-1-59615-118-5

Music Minus One

Exclusively Distributed By

HAL•LEONARD®

7777 W. Bluemound Rd. P.O. Box 3819 Milwaukee, WI 53213

Visit Hal Leonard Online at
www.halleonard.com

T0081723

Shiny Stockings

**Drum Charts by
Jim Chapin**

2

3

Satin Doll

6

Lil' Darlin'

Drummer should not play time on the bass drum behind Bass solo.

Girl Watchers Theme

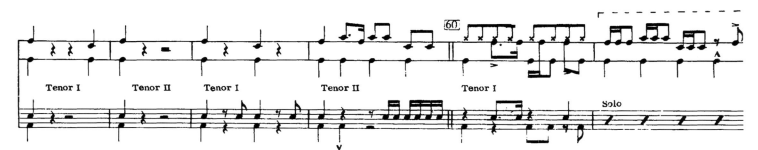

12

Wipe Out!

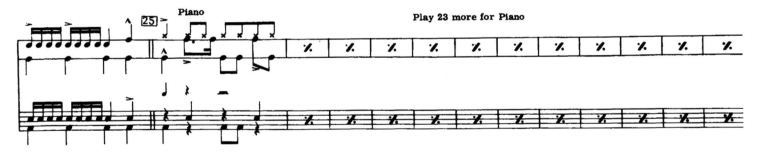

15

Sing, Sing, Sing

41

65

20

Cute

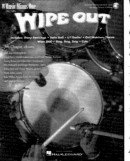